LIFE SKILLS

By Jason Coyne for VisionQuest

Goals for transition aged youth in semi-independent placement

jasoncoyne@outlook.com

Contents

HEALTH AND WELLNESS

Developing Healthy Habits

Meal Planning

Meal planning on a budget can be difficult but is completely achievable. Youth who have graduated from semi-independent living are accustomed to making independent grocery choices on a $50 weekly budget. They usually start out buying staples like bread and cold cuts, and plan more elaborate meals after a few more shopping trips when a larger supply of ingredients and seasonings are already stored at home. Some youth enjoy fruits and vegetables while others have to commit to including them in their basket. The foodbank can help fill the gap when budgeting on your own income.

United States Department of Agriculture
Center for Nutrition Policy and Promotion
Food Guide Pyramid
https://www.cnpp.usda.gov/FGP

Community Foodbank of Southern Arizona
http://www.communityfoodbank.org/

Hygiene and Fitness

According to the Center for Disease Control, teenagers and young adults should get one hour of exercise every day. Three days a week should include vigorous exercise like running and cycling. Many young adults join gyms, play sports, or visit the rec center to workout and socialize. Hiking is an activity that can be enjoyed alone or in a group.

Pima County
Natural Resources
Parks and Recreation
http://webcms.pima.gov/government/natural_resource
s_parks_and_recreation/

Arizona Smoker's Helpline
(800) 556-6222
http://www.ASHLine.org

Respite and Mental Health

While your primary care doctor looks after your physical health, your mental health is monitored by your psychiatrist or somebody else qualified from your clinical treatment team. Your PCP and mental healthcare provider often collaborate to maximize your health. A case manager or recovery coach usually supports the communication between you and your providers, so it is important to keep this person informed of how you are feeling. Starting or resuming services is as easy as calling the intake line at your Regional Behavioral Health Authority. You can immediately receive help for things like depression, drug use, anxiety, and stress.

Cenpatico Integrated Care
Customer Care 866-495-6738
Crisis 866-495-6735
How to Access Services
https://www.cenpaticointegratedcareaz.com/members
/how-to-access-services.html

NurseWise
Emergency Triage
(866) 495-6735

COPE Life in Full Throttle (LIFT)
Opioid Dependency Treatment Program
http://www.copecommunityservices.org/services/yout
h-services/life-in-full-throttle-lift/

Managing Medical Appointments

Reoccurring Appointments, Rescheduling Appointments and Medication Reviews

The calendar in your phone is a good place to put your doctor and dentist appointments as you make them. However, calendars are still available that hang on the wall or fit in your pocket. Youth who graduated from semi-independent living know how to schedule their annual or biannual appointments, and are able to call the office manager when needing to make a change. In addition to tracking the next appointment, it is a good idea to record when you need to re-enroll in coverage or benefits. This is a responsibility that starts the day you leave placement.

Arizona Health Care Cost Containment System (AHCCCS)

Young Adult Transitional Insurance (YATI)

https://www.azahcccs.gov/Members/GetCovered/Categories/YATI.html

Google Calendar

https://google.com/calendar

Outlook Calendar

https://office.live.com/start/Calendar.aspx

Urgent Care and Sudden Appointments

Getting sick is always unexpected and inconvenient. You could be sick enough to miss school or work and still be on the fence about calling your primary care doctor. Illness like this may merit a trip to a convenience clinic. They are located in your nearby pharmacy and can help more quickly. Still take a copy of your insurance coverage. For medical emergencies always call 911.

Walgreens Healthcare Clinic
https://www.walgreens.com/topic/pharmacy/healthcare-clinic.jsp

CVS Pharmacy Walk Ins
http://www.cvs.com/minuteclinic/

Labwork, Following up, Insurance and Accessing Benefits

Your doctor may ask you for labwork and it doesn't mean something is wrong. Labs help your doctor look inside your body more closely and determine what health risks and benefits they need to speak with you about. A lab order comes from your doctor and asks that you go to a lab location and possibly give blood, saliva, urine or something else; not at all painful except for a needle. Your doctor may tell you not to eat or drink for a length of time before submitting to labwork. That can help make the results clearer to read.

LabCorp
https://www.labcorp.com/

Sonora Quest Laboratories
https://www.sonoraquest.com/

Achieving Sexual Health

Health Resources

Practicing safe sex is an investment in your longterm health and wellbeing. Many of the clinics or case management buildings you already visit offer free condoms if you ask, as do your school and college. If you are uncomfortable outright asking the front desk for condoms then first ask to speak to a health liaison.

University of Arizona Health Department
Free Condoms Every Friday
https://uanews.arizona.edu/calendar/50291-free-condom-friday

Project Hard Hat
Free Condoms
https://www.projecthardhat.org/free-condoms.html

STDs

If you suspect you have an STD or want to begin routine testing, you can start by calling the health department's STD clinic at (520) 724-7900. You can expect to be treated with respect and made to feel comfortable through the process of submitting blood or urine and then waiting on results to return from the lab.

Pima County Health Department
STD Clinic
http://webcms.pima.gov/health/sexual_health/hiv_and_std/

SAAF Southern Arizona AIDS Foundation
http://saaf.org/hiv-prevention-and-testing/get-tested/

Pregnancy

If you or your significant other is pregnant, there are resources in the community that can help you access counseling, medical care and therapeutic support. There is professional help available to you at no cost that is knowledgeable on everything from abortion to prenatal care and birth control.

Teen Outreach Pregnancy Center
https://www.teenoutreachaz.org

Planned Parenthood
https://www.plannedparenthood.org/health-center

EDUCATION

Obtaining a High School Diploma or GED

Traditional, Charter, Online

Youth in semi-independent homes attend a variety of high schools. The traditional schools start around 8 in the morning and get out sometime around 3 in the afternoon. These schools have several teachers that cover all the core subjects and some electives. Youth who are behind in credits seem to like charter schools or credit recovery programs due to shorter hours, smaller classes, hands on teachers, and the possibility of simultaneous employment training. Curriculum administered entirely online is discouraged after witnessing too many failed attempts in program. Having teachers that know your name and let you access a library full of computers is a great personal resource! More on this later when you learn about your network and professional references. In lieu of a high school diploma, some youth pursue their GED which is a test that proves they have mastered a high school level education. This still requires studying and persistence but may also be a faster way to close a gap in education.

Tucson Unified School District
Most Recently Published Graduation Requirements
http://www.tusd1.org/contents/govboard/SectI/IKF.ht
ml

Youth on Their Own
Support for Students
https://yoto.org/

Ray Serrano
Community Engagement Specialist
PPEP Integrated Care
www.prepintegratedcare.com
901 E. 46th St, Tucson, AZ 85713
(520) 792-5704

GED Drop in Classes

Eckstrom-Columbus Library
Saturdays 1 p.m. to 4 p.m.

4350 E. 22nd St.
Tucson, AZ 85711

(520) 594-5285

Martha Cooper Library
Wednesdays 9 a.m. - 12 p.m.

1377 N. Catalina Ave.
Tucson, AZ 85712

(520) 594-5315

Pima Community College Adult Basic Education

To find out about becoming a PCC Adult Basic
Education student call (520) 206-3987 and talk with
an Adult Basic Education for College and Career
(ABECC) specialist. Specialists can tell you more
about programs and how and where to register for
classes.

Credits, Graduation and College Planning

High school graduation requires 21 credits from your core subjects and chosen interests accumulated through four years of school. For example, freshman math could be pre-algebra and sophomore math could be algebra. Similarly, the school probably won't let you take first year Spanish and then next year switch to first year Sign Language to satisfy the language requirement with two beginning subjects. Topics tend to build on themselves which is why consistency and attendance is important. Having to repeat a class doesn't create an insurmountable problem but missing a lot of school and having to repeat several classes can delay graduation. If you want to go to college then you should take stock of your credits and begin talking to your guidance counselor about your interests and goals.

Pima Community College

Admission and Registration Checklist

https://www.pima.edu/new-students/apply/how-to-apply.html

University of Arizona

How to Apply

https://admissions.arizona.edu/how-to-apply/freshmen

Workload and Resources

A lot of youth in semi-independent living are comfortable doing their homework in their rooms or at the kitchen table before bed. Other youth have to schedule doing their homework as soon as they come home or it will slip their mind as they transition into cooking dinner, watching TV and relaxing with their peers. Although your staff are very smart, they graduated from high school a long time ago so remember that the libraries all offer free tutoring on a schedule posted online and in person. The library tutors are very friendly and will take a look at anything you are working on. It is a good idea to seek additional help when you start to feel overwhelmed with schoolwork. Ask your teacher for their "office hours" which is time they designate certain days to meet with students one-on-one.

Pima County Library
Homework Help
https://www.library.pima.gov/teen-subject/tutoring/

College Options

Pima Community College and the University of Arizona

A high school diploma or GED is generally the prerequisite to get into your state college. Many youth start attending Pima Community College and then transfer to the University of Arizona when they are ready. The U of A accepts many credits from Pima. However, if you start at Pima and finish a degree program, the U of A will accept you as an established upperclassman and you won't have to take any freshman or sophomore classes. You can immediately start working on a bachelor's degree that interests you. College planning should start in your junior year of high school or as soon as you enter semi-independent living.

Pima Community College
https://pima.edu/

University of Arizona
http://www.arizona.edu/

Financial Aid, Scholarships, Transitions

There is one dedicated staff in the Department of Economic Services building at 22nd and Alvernon who helps you coordinate the payment of your in-state college education. As a youth in foster care, you can go to college and graduate at no cost to yourself. You set up a meeting with the DES education liaison through your assigned DCS specialist. Going to college out-of-state is not free but there are scholarships for which motivated students can apply. Although financial aid will cover the cost of your degree, the transition isn't without other challenges. Most college bound youth benefit from taking a campus tour of their intended university or community college way in advance of even enrolling. At college, the onus to get to class and finish work is much more of an independent responsibility than it was in high school.

U.S. Department of Education
Federal Student Aid
https://fafsa.ed.gov/

Workload and Resources

A traditional university experience is that you spend your time in class listening to a lecture and then work on a large project with a distant but approaching due date outside of class. Multiply that over the several courses you are taking and that is a lot of work you need to track, plan and remember. Graduating from college is very achievable, youth just like you work hard and graduate every year, but the job is made easier when you apply all of the skills you worked on in semi-independent living. Just like you did with your med reviews and benefits coverage, you can add project dates, the start and end of semesters, and study groups into your phone or planner. Often times in college, an important day is when class registration opens. Classes do fill up and some youth have had to wait an entire extra semester to take a course they need to graduate. A good idea is to stay ahead. One last thing about projects, is that in college you very often have to work in small groups of other students.

Ask for names and numbers and remember to stay involved.

University of Arizona
University Libraries
http://new.library.arizona.edu/

Non-College Options

Working and On-The-Job Training

Many youth take on part time jobs in semi-independent living. The program requires 30 to 40 hours a week of productivity with an emphasis on education. As youth work on high school or their GED, they may need more hours, they may legitimately like working, or they may just want income as the next step toward independence. Plenty of youth are non-college bound and that is OK but do keep in mind that staying in placement past the age of 18 carries a mandatory education requirement. Non-college bound youth typically leverage their high school education and work experience into higher paying jobs. Youth have graduated from semi-independent living while earning good pay in call centers, like Agero, and fast casual restaurants, like Beyond Bread. Each business offers advancement opportunities to its workers. Upward mobility is achieved more easily when youth update their resumes at each educational and employment milestone and stay connected to the more popular and reputable job seeking websites. Again, more on this later when you learn how to job search. While working, memorize how to access whatever pay portal or human resource website your employer uses so you can always print a paystub or performance related information. These records are important when you discharge and apply for subsidy!

LinkedIn
https://www.linkedin.com/

CareerBuilder
http://www.careerbuilder.com/

Trade School Certifications

Many youth have chosen to continue their education by completing a trade program and earning a certificate that employers like electricians, air conditioners, plumbers, landscapers, and many more look for when offering a high salary position. The youth do this by enrolling in a trade school. Job Corps is a comprehensive government grant program that Tucson is lucky to offer its youth. Job Corps is one such program that, as mentioned above, lets youth work on high school or their GED while learning a trade. Job Corps offers career training in automobile collision repair, retail management, construction, medical assisting and more. These certificates allow youth to directly enter the workforce and access more fulfilling work and higher salaries than they could with only a high school diploma. However, the program demands a lot from students and has a zero tolerance policy for drugs and alcohol. Recent changes at Job Corps has seen the implementation of advanced training options for youth who want to go even further in their specializations and trades. Youth who complete programs at the top of their class qualify to continue studying at Job Corps in other states. Each advanced training Job Corps has a unique relationship with its community. For example, if you go to Utah you can gain experience in forestry conservation and firefighting.

Fred G. Acosta
Job Corps Center
http://fredgacosta.jobcorps.gov/

Empire Beauty School
https://www.empire.edu/cosmetology-schools/arizona/tucson-university-area

Real Work Matters (RWM)
Tucson Vocational Schools, Trade Schools and Technical Schools
http://www.rwm.org/arizona/tucson/

Military

Some youth have expressed interest in joining the armed services after leaving semi-independent living which is a worthwhile goal that merits discussion with your CFT if applicable. After basic training, the military offers various careers in a myriad of fields like telecommunications, emergency medical, and engineering. All of the career paths require additional advanced education. The military can help you develop your interests and strengths, and offers substantial benefits to you and your family. You should include your team when meeting with a recruiter.

GoArmy
http://www.goarmy.com/

HOUSING AND TRANSPORTATION

Discharge Planning

Stable, Supportive and Proximity

Discharge planning starts the day you enter semi-independent living. For most, semi-independent is the last placement before living entirely as an independent adult. Turning 18 in placement shouldn't trigger a panic about where to live and with whom to live. Past residents have moved in with family, friends, coworkers and into their own apartments. When discussing your discharge location with your team, things to consider include continuity in your education program and where you may be working, how much of a commute you can comfortably take on, and where are the people with whom you enjoy spending the most time. Are your friends the most likely roommates to support your goals or will living with them cause a distraction? Is a coworker responsible enough to pay half of the bills if you agree to move in together? The choices you communicate to your team become part of your case for subsidy, which is the living stipend you earn from DCS for completing goals. This money helps you weather the transition and then slowly depreciates until you are surviving all by yourself. The next time you are leaving the grocery store, pick up a free apartment and housing guide and start envisioning where you might like to live after discharge.

Tucson Apartments
https://www.apartments.com/apartments/

Transitioning and Responsibility

When suddenly living on your own or with roommates, you will probably breathe a heavy sigh of relief that chores and the activities of daily living are now completed mostly on your terms. There will no longer be staff prompting you to remove your dirty dishes from your room or wake up on time for school. Hopefully your good habits are ingrained enough in your routine that you transition smoothly to getting everything done on your own. That isn't to say there won't ever be rules imposed on you again. Living in a rented space means you already agreed to certain rules or community standards. You won't be able to play music so loudly it wakes your neighbors or leave unsightly trash outside your front door because you didn't want to walk to the dumpster. Stay aware of the people living around you and aim to blend in with their common and courteous behavior. You also have the right to be treated fairly, and can escalate to your property manager if anybody in your new environment is harassing or causing you stress.

Continue soliciting advice from the team members helping you make this transition. Living on your own should definitely be a positive and rewarding experience.

Arizona Attorney General

Tenant's Rights and Responsibilities Handbook (Community Legal Services)

https://www.azag.gov/document/tenants-rights-and-responsibilities-handbook-community-legal-services

Expectations

In semi-indepenent living, youth are accustomed to the productivity schedule that includes a combination of school, work and volunteering to get to 30 to 40 hours a week. Whether you move in with relatives or friends, are still affiliated with the Arizona Young Adult Program or not, or living entirely on your own, you should have a conversation about expectations with the people in your life. Some youth have moved in with grandparents who wanted the work and schooling to continue on the schedule established in semi-independent. Other youth have moved in with friends who wanted to split all the bills and chores evenly. If you're setting out on your own, maybe you want to have a discussion with yourself and plan on holding yourself accountable to a schedule that includes not sleeping through your entire day off from work because the consequence for missing classes that day no longer feels as burdensome as it did with staff looming over you. Your expectations and goals are your own. Be assertive when collaborating to live with people, and make sure you pick those with whom you can depend. Also be dependable when you make promises. You want to enjoy where you live and keep strong relationships with those around you. When conflict comes up, you can use your healthy communication and problem solving skills or seek the help of mediators like landlords or social services.

Our Family Services
Free Family Mediation
http://www.ourfamilyservices.org/programs/prog005.
html

Mediation FAQ
http://www.ourfamilyservices.org/mediation-faq.html

Apartments and Housing

Section-8 and Payment Assistance

You are going to draw from your own income, your arrangement with your roommates, maybe subsidy, and possibly social services when paying for your living situation after discharge. Be aware that an older apartment with low rent may wind up costing you more in utilities because the air conditioner is older and has to really grind away all summer to keep you cool. Apartments with newer amenities may have lower bills because the appliances incorporate energy saving technology. The Department of Child Safety and the City of Tucson can offer help to you as you rent or lease your home. If you accepted subsidy then it means you were meeting your work and educational quota and have to continue to do so. If you accept rental assistance, affordable housing accommodations, or prepaid cash assist cards, it means you promised to accurately report your income and update your assets on record as they change. Participating in criminal activity or getting caught committing fraud or abuse could mean the loss of your housing agreement. Talk to your team and get online to explore all of the programs that can make living on your own more affordable.

City of Tucson

Section 8 Program Information

https://www.tucsonaz.gov/hcd/section-8-program-information

Rent, Insurance, Landlords, Guests

Rent is normally due on the first of the month with minor penalties for paying late within the first five days. After five days, fees can accumulate quickly. Your pay days at work most likely won't sync up with your bills and rent so stay vigilant about not spending the money you need to pay for rent, bills and essential expenses. In extreme cases, you can have a designated payee who receives your income and pays your bills before depositing the reminder into your discretionary spending account but as a graduate of semi-independent living that probably doesn't apply to you! Just stick to your budget and you'll be OK. As your friends visit you in your new home, have as much fun as possible and remind them that you're proud of the positive reputation you have with your neighbors and landlord. Several apartments ask that you disclose that you intend to allow a guest to crash on your couch or start living with you for a period longer than two weeks. Just keep an open mind and know that there are rules you're going to have to learn as you go. Did you know that pet rent is a thing? Sometimes bringing home a furry friend means spending an extra $5 - $20 a month which the landlord will use to replace the carpet if you ever move and he or she turns the unit over to somebody else. Again, if you feel taken advantage of it is a good idea to solicit advice from the knowledgeable sources that helped you transition. You can also protect the items in your new home from fire, flood and theft by purchasing different amounts of renter's insurance.

University of Arizona
Student Legal Services (Landlord Tips)
http://legal.asua.arizona.edu/Legal_Services/home.html

Allstate
https://www.allstate.com/renters-insurance.aspx

Statefarm
https://www.statefarm.com/insurance/home-and-property/renters

Furniture, Utilities, Maintenance, Repair, Moving

Moving around is a fact of life and doesn't always have to be stressful. Whether you're moving into your first place or a new place, there are some services you're going to have to set up and some services you're going to want to set up. Apartments that don't provide utilities for free will usually give you about five days worth of electricity with an expectation that you call Tucson Electric Power and get an account set up in your name. That WiFi you enjoyed in semi-independent living? Now you're going to have to call Cox or Comcast and pay for that. Getting Internet at home requires a monthly service subscription and some hardware, usually a modem and a router, but sometimes a combination of both in one device. The Internet Service Providers also called ISPs will offer you their hardware to rent but with a small amount of technical know how it is almost always more economical to purchase your own from Walmart or Target. Every time you move you will need to notify your utility companies so they can transfer your services to your new home, usually on the same account. Easy! People move every day and it isn't a big deal. As things like faucets, door handles, dishwashers, laundry machines, and air conditioners wear out or break, notify your landlord who will send a maintenance technician to help you. You're probably on your own for something small like a burned out light bulb. It is a good idea to know what the after hours emergency phone number is for burst pipes and the like before you need it but listening to the voicemail that plays when you call your apartments after the leasing office is closed will also probably tell you. If your team hasn't already helped you find affordable furniture for your new place, take a look at your budget and consider Goodwill, thrift stores, garage sales, and pieces you assemble yourself from Big Lots! and Family Dollar. For starters, you need a bed, a table, some chairs, a desk and an entertainment stand. The bed will need sheets, and you'll need a towel to dry off with after showering. You won't think of everything right away but set aside some money to make purchases as you go. A pillow and laundry basket are probably purchases that come before tropical fishtanks and pinball machines but with budgeting and planning you will add everything you need in your new home.

Pima County
Utility Assistance
http://webcms.pima.gov/community/help_now/utility
_assistance/

Goodwill of Southern Arizona
http://www.goodwillsouthernaz.org/

Tucson Electric Power
https://www.tep.com/

Comcast
https://www.xfinity.com/

Transportation

Permits and Licenses

Many driven youth ask their teams about getting their driver's license because they know getting around on their own will be easier with a car. Although semi-independent staff can't teach you to drive (though they can help you understand the fundamentals as you ride around with them) your DCS specialist can request funds to pay for lessons. Your team usually asks you to do the legwork and find a driving school that looks good to you. Once you print the pricing packages and your workers get the classes approved you can graduate from a driving school. Successfully completing a driving school usually means you receive a voucher which you exchange for a driver's license. If you have to take the road test so be it just relax and do your best. Driving is a skill that takes practice and something you will be refining your whole life as a motorist. A hot tip is that unlike the other Motor Vehicle Divisions in town that conclude the road test with parallel parking, the MVD on 22nd and Sarnoff only makes you do a three point turn (look it up). However, none of this happens, not even the lessons, until you get your permit. You need to go into an MVD near you or log onto the website to receive and review the Arizona Department of Transportation study manual. All you do is study and pass a written test. You hardly need staff involvement to get started, so what are you waiting for? If you want to drive then start studying the manual.

Arizona Department of Transportation
http://www.azdot.gov/

AZDOT Study Manual
https://www.azdot.gov/docs/default-source/mvd-forms-pubs/99-0117.pdf

Car Insurance, Registration and Emissions

If you started looking at cars or are even relying on your common sense alone, you know that getting behind the wheel has costs. Buying a cheaper automobile may mean you pay more in maintenance later. Hopefully, at this step you have some money in your savings account. Consulting the Kelley Blue Book can help you research the value of used cars. Once you own a car, which you legally have to insure, you also pay an annual registration fee. Your participation in driving means you have a responsibility to help pay for the roads and clean air by way of these fees you encounter. You will also need an oil change after so many miles, which keeps your engine lubricated, and of course living in Arizona means the dry climate will wear your tires out faster than you'd like. Since you live on your own and get a lot of advertising delivered to your mailbox every day, keep an eye out for coupons at local service stations like Jiffy Lube and BrakeMAX.

Going to the same garage for maintenance over and over establishes a relationship between you and the business and you might get better service. The technician will also come to learn the quirks of your vehicle and if your car breaks down you may save more money getting to the root of the problem more quickly.

Service Arizona
Vehicle Services Online
http://servicearizona.com/

Official Kelley Blue Book
Research Car Values
https://www.kbb.com/

Geico
https://www.geico.com

Big O Tires
https://www.bigotires.com/

Bikes, Busses, Ride Sharing and Flying

By necessity, every youth in semi-independent living immediately becomes a proficient public transporter. Many youth don't mind the bus while others loathe it. The bus system is convenient but almost no youth actually love taking the bus. However, if you're not ready for a car when you leave the program the bus will still be there for you. Depending on the services you discharge with, you may have to provide your own monthly bus pass. There is money to save by going to the bus station and purchasing a refillable pass or applying for reduced rates versus just boarding and paying for each ride. You will have to figure out what works for you and your budget. You may have used a grant from Arizona Friends of Foster Care to acquire a bicycle while in semi-independent living in which case that bike is yours to keep. If you find your bike needing maintenance then there are plenty of shops that can help you. Maybe you only need to see a tire changed a few times before you feel comfortable paying less and changing it on your own. Getting from point A to point B can be accomplished any number of ways, and all you can do is practice, learn your streets, and utilize all the navigation tools technology offers these days. When receiving directions by phone, a good question to ask the representative is, "What are your crossroads?" If you're on 22nd St. looking for the Motor Vehicle Division on Sarnoff Dr. then maybe it is helpful to know it is after Kolb but before Houghton on the right when traveling east. Can you establish the direction you're facing without a compass? The sun rises in the east and sets in the west. Can you recognize the Santa Catalina mountain range north of you? A lot of youth these days are using Uber and Lyft via their smartphones to get around. Maybe apps are economical for special travel needs or finding a new destination for the first time. Just like anything else, flying on an airplane may be intimidating the first time but ask questions and read signs. Take note before landing, most places won't rent you a car until you're older than 25.

Sun Tran App Center
Navigation Tools
http://www.suntran.com/developers_showcase.php

Arizona Friends of Foster Children Foundation
http://www.affcf.org/

Performance Bicycle
http://www.performancebike.com/bike-shop/store/tucson

Priceline
Flights, Hotels, Rental Cars
https://www.priceline.com

EMPLOYMENT

Job Search Preparations

Assembling Accomplishments and References

Nearly all youth in semi-independent living start building income for living on their own, even if they are just finishing school and planning to apply for subsidy. Moving into semi is also when a lot of youth go from relying on staff to always have their necessary documentation to carrying copies of their own important papers. You should ask for a solid binder and start keeping and organizing everything you need to start memberships, join programs, apply for benefits, and begin working in the community. If you anticipate getting a job then you can expect to need an original copy of your birth certificate or a social security card. Hopefully you have one or the other as they can each be used to acquire the one you don't have. Don't panic if you have neither, you will just need your team's support to request them. You may already have a state ID, which by now is a must have in your life. If you don't have a state ID then get the $12 from your DCS specialist and go to the MVD with three forms of identification (in this case, a school ID is OK as long as the other two are your birth certificate and social security card). With getting a job in mind, plan on always having copies of your academic transcripts. Put your high school diploma someplace safe as soon as you earn it. Save any awards you receive from your school because those accomplishments can entice businesses to hire you while you lack prior work experience. Teachers with whom you worked particularly well can also write you letters of recommendation. In fact, even if you aren't applying for a job, you'd do well to ask a teacher you like to write you a general letter of recommendation at the end of the semester. There will come a point in time when you do need somebody established in their field to vouch for you and teachers make excellent references. Any documentation you discover missing can be reacquired from its source but you may encounter fees. Some youth decide to keep digital copies of their important records in Google Docs or Dropbox.

Need My Transcript

(Shipping and Handling Fees – First try contacting your high school on your own)

https://needmytranscript.com/

Pima County Office of Vital Records

Obtaining a Birth Certificate

http://webcms.pima.gov/health/personal_records/birth_death_certificates/

Social Security Office

3808 N. 1st Ave.

Tucson, AZ 85719

(800) 772-1213

Creating and Polishing a Resume

A resume is a summary of your work history and skills contained to a single piece of paper. This is a snapshot of what you have to offer a company for whom you'd like to work. If you don't have a lot of work experience then you may struggle to think of what you should put on a resume. Keep in mind not all jobs are work you were hired into. Some youth have been successful finding work in the community by filling out a resume that highlights volunteer programs they were a part of in placement, clubs they facilitated in school, or errands they did for their family. If all you've done is been paid $20 for cleaning out yards and garages then that is what you are going to put on your resume. A resume isn't set in stone, and you should save yours somewhere on a USB drive or in the cloud so you can add to it every time you graduate from a program or start working somewhere new. Again, you can still feel good about a resume that is a little light. Everybody has to establish themselves over time. That's why references from your staff and teachers can go a long way in helping you find initial employment. Although you could probably sit at a computer facing a blank document and come up with a decent resume knowing only that it needs your contact information and a list of work and school accomplishments, it doesn't hurt to review some free templates available online. There are lots of styles so choose the settings that suit your information. If your phone service cuts in and out for non-payment, consider giving the phone number at your placement. If your email address sounds unconventional (gangsta_player), consider registering a new one that is just your name. Take heart, you're going to pour work into your resume and then have to repeat yourself when applying for jobs online. That's just the way it is! At least having your resume makes recalling your information more convenient for you. A byproduct of registering on job search websites is that some take your answers and create a resume for you. You'll need to feel ownership of your resume and be able to change it when you need to, so decide if using a resume building tool is better than firing up your preferred word processor. If you do not have access to a computer in placement you will need to visit your school or the library. Many youth have attempted a resume on their phones and quickly realized that although possible this route isn't ideal. The library even offers specific hours for help with resumes! Just consult the calendar or ask a librarian.

Microsoft Office
Resume Templates
https://templates.office.com/en-us/Resumes-and-Cover-Letters

Networking Friends and Acquaintances

Finding a job from somebody you know isn't just a feature for youth living in a semi-independent placement. Many people enter their jobs because they learned about an opening from someone they know already working there. Businesses often times like to hire acquaintances of their established employees because they can usually count on the new hire being about as honest, loyal and effective as the person already working there. This is because people tend to associate with those whose values and interests are similar to their own. Youth in semi have come home and announced that places where they are working are looking for more help. If this is your point of entry into a new job, appreciate that your friend put his or her reputation on the line by recommending you. Try and become an asset to the company by offering your best work. Often times companies will reward references that work out well for them with bonuses paid to their original employee. You might help somebody you know get a job some day and earn money for doing so. Be aware of scams, though. If the company somebody from your social circle is recommending doesn't ask for any of the above mentioned documents and isn't a place with a logo you recognize then you may want to consult your team or check its validity online. There are unfortunately various schemes aimed at taking advantage of job seekers. Never pay money to begin a new job. While mining your network of friends, family, staff and teachers for job openings, you may hear of job fairs, hiring events, open interviews, and grand openings. Participating in as many of these opportunities as you can may help you land a job before any stressful searching but can also expand your network and yield additional opportunities in the future. As you put yourself out there, you may want to review what social media turns up when you google yourself, and set certain posts to private if you think they may hinder your job search. Keeping a job related profile online may redirect attention away from content you regret but can't remove. Your network is bigger than you think it is, and if you know somebody who likes working then ask them if their job is hiring.

Better Business Bureau of Southern Arizona
http://www.bbb.org/tucson/

About Me
https://about.me/

Job Searching

Finding Openings and Checking Job Boards

Beginning a job search from scratch can feel overwhelming, especially if you have never committed to looking before. However, take solace knowing that almost everyone who has a job today went through this process, too. The best place to start looking for a job is in the areas surrounding your placement. If somebody in a business reacts strongly to learning more about you, consider the following scenarios. There are businesses close to your placement that recognize your address and have had positive past experiences from youth working there, and, unfortunately, some businesses have come to know your placement from past youth giving them negative experiences. If you maintain a positive attitude and get hired, you may well turn around what the company thinks of your placement and make getting a job easier for a youth that comes after you. Fear not, most businesses have no idea that your address is anything other than a house but be aware that youth do tend to apply at the same places and it has happened that a local business recognized the address. Most youth are hard workers and by reputation semi-independent youth get and keep jobs. You have that going for you. Other places to search for job openings are websites. You can log onto Craigslist and start looking at jobs immediately, usually applying by attaching your resume to an email. Or you can use a site like Jobing which has a signup process followed by applying for jobs via its links and submission fields. Taking notes is a really good idea while applying for jobs in your community. Often times you will speak to the first employee you see walking into a business and they may tell you that a manager won't be in until tomorrow. That would be a good reminder to jot down. If you come back the next day and remember that employee's name and say hi to them then they may comment that you are friendly and assertive when they get their manager. A manager is nine times out of ten going to thank you for coming in and ask you to go home and fill out an application online. You didn't waste your time by going in. If you apply that same night then the manager will likely remember you from the in person encounter. Meeting you provided the manager with a positive first impression, and he or she will read your resume to learn more about you. When looking for a job, you can never do enough. Don't stop at submitting one application or after your first positive experience with a manager. Many leads can go nowhere and it doesn't mean you did anything wrong. There are many, many people looking for jobs!

Jobing
http://tucson.jobing.com

Craigslist
https://tucson.craigslist.org/

Cover Letters

You found an enticing job and you're ready to send your resume. While a resume is that snapshot of your work history, completed education, and special skills, a cover letter is another single piece of paper you write that tells this specific business why you especially want to work there. Many online job applications have an attachment button that lets you upload a resume, cover letter, and other relevant documents (like a food handlers certification) while others do not. If you really want a job for which you are applying and its online form doesn't allow attachments, you aren't breaking any unwritten rules by showing up the next day with your supporting documents printed out. Just say you'd like the following papers to be included with your application and hand them over. A successful cover letter is a concise explanation why you want this job and how your skill set makes you a proper candidate for this job. For example, if you'd like to work in a pet store maybe your cover letter would say you took care of a variety of pets from a young age and learned enough about each one so that you could intelligently discuss their diets and nutrition with customers. You may mention that you consistently volunteered with Pima Paws or Greyhound Adoption for six months. Although you don't know anything about grooming, you may mention that if hired for retail sales you would maintain an interest in learning more about the store's pet salon. Suddenly your potential manager knows you have some relevant experience, some desire to grow in the industry, and some staying power as you mentioned how the job aligns with your interests. Taking care to include a good cover letter can really set your application apart from the rest.

Monster.com
5 simple steps to writing a successful cover letter
https://www.monster.com/career-advice/article/5-simple-steps-to-a-successful-cover-letter-hot-jobs

Applying, Interviewing and Following Up

You assembled your documentation, made a resume, networked your friends, searched for jobs, found some openings, and wrote out thoughtful cover letters. If you haven't already applied for the jobs you want then you will have to do so now. Filling out job applications online is not normally fun and several youth have dropped out at this stage, having to regroup and come back when they are more mentally prepared for what can be a long and unappealing process. In addition to several pages asking for the same information included on your resume, many online job applications include an aptitude test. These online exams are purportedly there to provide hiring managers with a computer determined summary of what type of employee you'd make. The jury is still out on how effective these computer tests are at picking successful employees but if you don't want this test to be the only thing your potential boss knows about you then be sure you make that in store appearance count and submit your nice looking resume and cover letter. An online aptitude test taken with a job application may ask a question like: Are you always on time or do you always doublecheck your work? That is definitely a confusing question and there might not be a right answer. Obviously, being punctual is important but so is performing a task correctly. The algorithm that assesses your answers looks for patterns in how you answer these sometimes aggravating questions and guesses at your best working traits. It's OK to rely on your gut and move through these questions quickly. If this test is going to sink you in this one instance then there is nothing you can do about it. You can help yourself a lot more by pouring additional effort into your face-to-face encounters, your resume and especially your cover letter. Getting asked to interview allows you the opportunity to show rather than tell all the things you have been selling about yourself in the application process. You may want to grab a staff and act out a mock interview, which is your staff playing the part of the interviewer and asking you several questions that will come up in the actual interview. Succinct answers are usually best and it is OK to say you don't know something but want to learn. Offer handshakes, maintain eye contact, and have at least a couple questions of your own ready as you will probably be asked if you have any at the end of the interview. If you have not heard about a job you applied for or even interviewed for then it is appropriate to follow up by phone or in person about once a week. An old practice was to send a courteous note after being interviewed. This isn't done as much today but if you particularly enjoyed the opportunity to interview somewhere you may consider sending a thank you card. If you get disappointing news from somewhere you really want to work, ask if there is anything you can do within the next six months to make yourself a more appealing candidate and consider reapplying.

Free Printable Thank You Cards
https://printable-cards.gotfreecards.com/categories/thank-you

United States Postal Service
Addressing Your Mail
http://pe.usps.com/text/dmm100/addressing-mail.htm

Maintaining Employment

The Grind and How to Quit

Getting a job is exciting and getting paid is probably more exciting. However, having a job just to get paid may turn into a grind after awhile. Having to put on a uniform and go to work over and over may become tiring, and you may remember how freeing it felt to come home from school and have the entire rest of the day clear for relaxation and fun with your housemates. Maybe you even met your savings goal. If you really don't want to do something then there are many ways your mind will talk you out of doing it any longer. Whatever you do, don't just walk out and quit. You worked hard to get this job and if it really isn't for you then you owe it to yourself (and especially your future job seeking self) to end the working relationship correctly. A boring adult you know may have said something like work is work or it would be called play. It's a stupid phrase but somewhat true. Not everybody will find their dream job immediately. Many people will work several jobs all the while calculating how they will arrive at their dream job. In addition to your job paying you, your job is also compensating you in work experience or your ability to show your next employer that you did a good job and you did so for an amount of time that was beneficial to the company. If you really can't stand a new job, is it at least tolerable enough to do for six months? Six months is a decent length of time to learn how to start a new job, learn how to acclimate to a company's culture, learn how to observe coworkers, learn how to interact with customers, learn how to follow a routine but pivot to an unexpected assignment, and generally learn how to act professional in the workplace. Six months is also probably the minimum amount of time you want to show on a resume that you worked for the same company (unless it was an internship). Six months tells your next employer that you probably won't quit the next day, and your new cover letter may even mention what you learned in your last job that makes you even more excited about your next job. While resigning from a job, it is customary to do so in writing and promise to work two more weeks. This is called your two weeks' notice. You want to stay in your old boss's good graces by giving them enough time to hire and train somebody else. When they hired you they likely relaxed thinking that position was filled for the time being. If you tried your best then you shouldn't feel too badly about quitting a job that wasn't right for you. Thank your manager and coworkers for the experience and move on. You're always going to be trying to strike a better balance between work and life. Colloquially, that means you consciously decide how much time and energy you're going to exert into work and how much you're going to save for home and hobbies.

Salary.com
14 Steps to Achieving Work-Life Balance
http://www.salary.com/14-steps-to-achieving-work-life-balance/

Forbes.com

6 Tips For Better Work-Life Balance

https://www.forbes.com/sites/deborahlee/2014/10/20/
6-tips-for-better-work-life-balance/

US NEWS Money

How to Quit Your Job like a Class Act

http://money.usnews.com/money/careers/slideshows/
how-to-quit-your-job-like-a-class-act

Work Ethic and Fun

Going to work shouldn't be the end of having fun. You're now going to have to develop a work ethic that fits your personality. If you enjoy the social aspect of going to school and can do the work while there, you may very well enjoy your job. A part time job while living in a semi-independent placement should complement what you're already doing and reflect your interests and goals. Youth in the past have taken up jobs just to have a pro-social activity for part of the weekend and extend employee discounts on coveted items like basketball sneakers to their friends and family. Aside from some deadly serious workers wanting to save enough money to move into their own apartments as soon as possible, lots of youth make their first foray into part time employment over summer vacation. There are youth who are already established in their part time jobs, which have been pizza places and retail stores, who can stop working when school starts and then easily re-apply and pick up the same job the following summer. A part time job to cover copious amounts of downtime is a great idea, and you will be better prepared to apply for a job you really want, perhaps one the aligns with your ongoing education and desired career, as you transition from semi to full independence. The idea in its simplest form is that you have something productive to show for your time spent in semi-independent living. The truth is, you can become indispensable at your job very easily. Just perform your task to the best of your ability and keep an eye out for anything else that needs to be finished before a shift ends. One youth working at Fry's went from pushing carts to decorating cakes, a significant raise, just because they saw the manager struggling with a new display and went over to help. Straight A high school students don't always make the best workers. Sometimes a student who goes to school and makes average marks, hangs with a good group of friends, shows a sharp sense of humor, develops some hobbies, and is observant in their environment is better suited to leave a lasting impression at a part time job. This well balanced and positive youth is making connections that will ensure they get a job whenever they need one, always moving into higher paid and more stimulating positions. For this youth, work ethic means performing their job duties to the best of their ability while there and rewarding themselves when finished for the day.

LifeHack
How to Build a Reliable Work Ethic
http://www.lifehack.org/articles/featured/how-to-build-a-reliable-work-ethic.html

Promotions and Turning Hard Work into New Opportunity

When the days turn into weeks, months and years, at even part time jobs, you really become a reputable worker with diverse employment opportunities. Many entry level employers like roadside assistance call centers boast that most of upper management started out on the phones. Walmart and Target also like to tell new hires in orientation that many store managers started by completing an application at an in store hiring kiosk and then went on to learn each unique area of the store. Having an employment goal in mind may make the grind more palatable. If you want to become a manager, perhaps inform your current manager at your 90 day evaluation that this is your goal and your responsibilities can be expanded to include more of what you will need to know to advance. Some companies, like Enterprise, outright solicit candidates who are willing to start at the bottom and work their way up. Though, in this example, Enterprise requires a college degree and advertises that its management training program unfolds at an accelerated pace. But working anywhere, under any circumstance, does create opportunity for advancement. One youth struggled to find gainful employment and so kept going back to their library internship to stay busy until landing a job that allowed them to graduate from the semi-independent program making more money than their staff (and without a high school diploma)! This youth enjoyed working nights so as to sleep and play video games during the day. This youth responded positively to their company's one month intensive training program and made an employment goal of becoming a company trainer. At last check in, a year later, this youth had worked for the same company they found while in semi-independent placement and had already received a raise and the opportunity to take on some training responsibilities. If you work hard, meet people, take the steps needed to improve, and build your resume then you can accomplish your employment goals. Of note, E-Learning is a quick way to add experience to your resume. Browse the Internet for topics you can, for free, quickly master and then download a certificate of completion. Computer skills are always in demand, and emergency management training always looks good at any company.

Federal Emergency Management Agency
Distance Learning and Self Paced Courses
https://training.fema.gov/is/

Code Academy
Learn to Code for Free
https://www.codecademy.com/

Open Culture
The Best Free Cultural and Educational Media on the Web
http://www.openculture.com/free_certificate_courses

Enterprise Trainee Program
https://careers.enterprise.com/management-trainee

Enterprise Management Program
http://go.enterpriseholdings.com/opportunities/management-training-program/

BANKING AND SAVING

Opening a Bank Account

Finding a Bank

Finding a bank is easy, you probably know where several of them are already. If you're 18 then you can just walk right in and speak with a banker about opening an account. A greeter will probably help you as soon as you enter, if not, put your name on the sign in sheet and wait to be called. You'll have to deposit an initial amount, usually $100, and then you'll be on your way in under an hour. Your new bank card and additional instructions will arrive in the mail. From there, you can start making transactions through the teller window, ATMs, which stand for Automatic Teller Machines, and various vending services online. Having a bank account is important for protecting your money. Youth who cash their paychecks find that the money burns a hole in their pocket quickly. That's not to say youth with bank accounts don't succumb to frivolous purchases but they seem more aware of their income and enjoy watching their balance grow. If you win a dispute with a seller then the bank can also electronically reverse a bad transaction. In recent times, banks have made it more difficult for youth who are under 18 to open their own accounts, that is, having the account in only their name. Until DCS responds in some way, you may not be able to open a bank account of your own until you turn 18. If you have a family member willing to co-sign for the new account you may choose to accept their assistance. Be responsible with your bank account, especially if someone else's name is also attached to it.

Chase
(high school accounts confirmed)
https://www.chase.com/

WellsFargo
https://www.wellsfargo.com/

Bank of America

https://www.bankofamerica.com/

Considering a Credit Union

Some youth open their first money accounts at credit unions. You may have even received advice that a credit union is better than a bank. You can educate yourself on the topic and choose for yourself. Some people prefer credit unions because they offer the same services as banks but can offer lower fees on services and higher interest rates on savings. Whereas banks operate for profit, credit unions are not for profit. A credit union is owned by its members and any money earned goes back into itself or is paid out to its members. You may be able to get a more enticing loan at a credit union. Reasons some consumers might not choose a credit union include fewer branches, membership fees, difficulty finding an ATM, early withdrawal penalties (you would be expected to save your money and not touch it until a certain date or amount---which is good for you and the credit union because you will make more money but you might actually need it sooner due to an unforeseen circumstance), less interactive websites, inability to handle complex banking needs (probably doesn't apply to you at this stage in your financial life), and the possibility of not surviving as a small business. Youth in semi-independent living report satisfaction using both banks and credit unions. Youth appear to choose banks more often primarily for the convenience. There's probably a commercial bank operating right out of your grocery store.

Hughes Credit Union
(high school accounts confirmed)
https://www.hughesfcu.org/

Tucson Federal Credit Union
https://www.tucsonfcu.com/

Pima Federal Credit Union
http://www.pimafederal.org/

Establishing Credit and Banking History

Do you feel like an adult now with a job and a bank account, and what is all this responsibility providing for you? Your job probably offers or even requires direct deposit. New hire paperwork probably asked that you submit a voided check. To void a check just write "void" across the line meant for a dollar amount. Your human resource department will take your bank account and routing number from the check so payroll can deposit your income every payday. Depending on what you intend to do with your money, you may want a portion of your paycheck sent right to your savings account, which is separate from your checking account. You can set this up with a teller or through the user portal on your bank's website. The benefit is that you won't accidentally spend what you intend to save. You're doing all this because some day you may want to purchase a car, house, or additional education by asking for a loan or financing and you will need to show your bank or credit union that you are a safe risk and a good investment (think of why you would feel safer lending some of your friends money over others and the answer probably comes down to who has established your trust). A loan officer will look at your banking history and see that you steadily receive income, save a portion, and pay your bills on time. Of course you need to try and make your loan payments timely so as to not trigger penalties and higher interest rates. Similarly, you may have a credit card by now. If you work full time for minimum wage, you may have accepted an offer for a small line of credit. Let's say you received a $1,500 line of credit. What do you do with this? Hopefully you are surviving on your carefully planned budget until, suddenly, life happens. You drove over a hazard on the road and your car needs work. The $600 in car repairs doesn't fit into your budget so you use your credit card. Now you have $900 left to spend on your credit card, and a $600 balance that needs to be paid off. That balance is also accruing interest, as in, you are charged a small (at first) continually growing fee for making purchases with credit instead of money.

Whoever issued your credit card will start asking for a minimum monthly payment. Laws require the paperwork to tell you how much extra money (interest) you would pay back by making the minimum monthly payment. If you make the minimum monthly payments on your credit card, depending on the interest specified in your contract, you may end up paying back $700, $800 or more on that $600 you used to fix your car. Even paying back a little over the monthly minimum is a good idea. Going into debt is easy, and most people are, to varying degrees, in debt. But that statistic doesn't have to include you! Be aware that how you use your money and credit has consequences, good and bad, and do your best.

Federal Trade Commission
Get My Free Credit Report
https://www.ftc.gov/faq/consumer-protection/get-my-free-credit-report

Banking Tools

Checks, Money Orders, Bill Pay

Youth move into semi-independent placement with all kinds of smartphones, tablets and laptops. These devices make our lives easier and afford us a whole lot of fun but please educate yourself on the hidden costs. For example, an Amazon Fire Tablet is exceptionally cheap for such a powerful and amazing tablet. Amazon loses money when it sells this hardware at that low of a price. Amazon does this because it counts on you spending more money on its goods and services than you would if you didn't own the tablet. You may want to go into your device settings and disable one-click purchasing. Tapping a screen to make a purchase is more impulsive than handing over cash or swiping a bank card in a store, and many people buy things they don't need just because of how easy and painless online shopping has made spending money. Staff usually comment or facilitate a group in semi-independent placement when they notice an alarming number of packages youth ordered arriving at the doorstep. With those warnings out of the way, the good news is that banking tools today are very helpful! Youth currently living in semi-independent are using their phones to access modern banking services such as automatic bill pay, money transfers, and check cashing. One youth takes a picture of the check his internship prints for him in exchange for his good grades, and the money is automatically deposited into his account. There will be times when you can't complete a task online. If you write a check, be mindful of your bank balance and leave enough money in the account so that the check clears. If you write a $50 check because you have $60 in your bank account, but then spend $20 before the check clears, your check will bounce. You could get charged a penalty, you will still owe $50 to whoever you wrote the check to, and you may be a little embarrassed. If you haven't built up a healthy bank balance, consider using a money order instead of a check. You will inform the bank teller that you need to pay somebody $50 and the teller will deduct it from your $60 and give you a piece of paper that looks like the check but carries that bank's promise of $60. Now your account reflects the $10 you actually have left to spend and you may not make the same mistake. A check or money order is there because you typically don't send cash through the mail except in birthday cards. People used to balance their checkbook with pen and paper more than they do today. As you comfortably rely on your banking apps, sharpen your awareness of how long certain transactions take to process. The number you're looking at on your screen representing the amount of money you have in your account may have another deposit or withdrawal waiting in queue.

PayPal
https://www.paypal.com

Tellers and ATMs

You're going to visit ATMs and live tellers for your banking needs. Your DCS specialist most likely told you that there are matching money rewards for keeping a balance in your savings account. Youth in placement have entered deals where having $500 in their savings account by the time they graduate means DCS will pay them an additional $1,000 for being responsible. You may be a youth who is moderately successful saving money but then a fun opportunity, like a concert, comes up with friends and you suddenly want to tap a small amount of savings to cover the cost. That's OK! If you're moderately successful at saving money and are aware that you used a portion of your savings for an excursion with friends then you will probably make efforts to pay back your savings more quickly when you don't have an activity planned with friends. All of these transactions can be handled inside the bank and many of them can be performed outside the bank. ATMs are scattered all over town and you can usually keep your eyes peeled and find an ATM that belongs to your bank. You can usually use another bank's ATM for a small fee. You'll find nondescript ATMs in places like gas stations and movie theaters. These ATMs usually charge fees larger than what you would encounter using an ATM from a bank other than your own. A nondescript ATM may still be convenient or even necessary for whatever you're trying to do in the moment. If your car breaks down and the tow truck driver requires cash, you may have to use the most readily available ATM which could be in the gas station across the street. In this position, you may make the creative decision to purchase a pack of gum and ask the cashier for cash back. Cash back is a service offered in places like grocery and convenience stores where you can be charged the sum of the items you're buying and an additional amount over your total which you will receive back in the form of dollars and change. In this scenario, you may need $40 in cash so you buy a pack of gum for a dollar. Your card will be swiped for $41 dollars and then the cashier will hand you your gum, your receipt, and your two twenty dollar bills. If you arrive at an

ATM with a line, be patient, most people do not spend very long using an ATM. Be courteous and stand far enough back that the person you're waiting on doesn't feel like you are spying on their keypad selections or feeling like you might rob them. Also be aware that criminals can manipulate ATMs to steal access to your bank accounts. For extra comfort, you could gently pull on the card reader before sliding in your card to make sure no fraudulent hardware has been added to the ATM. You'll never be completely safe, as banking information can also be stolen via bluetooth enabled devices that criminals use to constantly skim public places where people use their apps, but you can stay aware and report any suspicious activity as quickly as possible. The faster you notice something went wrong the more likely your bank can correct the problem. If you didn't have a bank account and were straight up robbed of your cash then there'd be a much smaller chance of getting your money back. Good thing you're a modern and independent minded young person!

VISA

Global ATM Locator

www.visa.com/atmlocator/index.jsp

Rewards

Remember that $600 credit purchase you needed to make to repair your car? Let's say you got back on the road safely and by paying more than the minimum monthly payments you paid your balance off quickly and way before that $600 turned into a larger and less manageable amount. If this incident were real, depending on your credit card, you may have earned some points from a benefits program associated with your credit card. Some young adults who were previously youth in a semi-independent placement may choose to use their credit cards for more than emergencies because of the various rewards programs. Using a credit card for daily life coupled with the ability to actually pay off the balance every month may make sense if you're earning rewards. Rewards could be anything from cash, movie tickets, dinners, and trips. If you're responsible with your money and the master of your budget then you may very well benefit from engaging in a credit card reward program. However, like with your inexpensive tablet, just know that companies aim to make money. The rewards are enticing because credit card companies make money when consumers start missing payments and owing more than that which they bargained. This information isn't to persuade you to seek out a credit card reward program but to inform you of how other youth and young adults have used money services. Earned rewards can be rescinded or taken away once a customer falls behind on payments. You may prefer seeking a reward program that doesn't hinge on spending money. Despite a lot of spam advertisements, there are genuine websites that will pay you to take surveys. Some youth have incorporated survey taking toolbars into their web browsing and earned money and goods. Do your research and consult people you trust. In a pinch, if you're trying to decide if the imaginary to this example website 'Windfall Survey' is reputable, google "Is Windfall Survey real or fake?" or "Does Windfall Survey work?" and read reviews from other users. Whatever you're trying to do, other people tried it first and then shared about the experience. You can find the best reward programs by experimentation and reading the experiences of others. Keep an eye out for other ways to make money. An entrepreneurial youth added a revenue stream when they started cleaning fish tanks at dental offices. Hard work and innovative thinking often yield financial reward.

Swagbucks
https://www.swagbucks.com

Amazon
http://www.amazon.com

eBay
http://www.ebay.com

Setting Goals for Money

Financial Planning

Some sensible youth in semi-independent living have decided that the difference between their income and their allowance is that one is for saving and the other is for having fun. Your placement may save your DCS allowance for you in an account with other residents' allowances so that you discharge with a decent amount of money. That is your money and you can request it at any time. Some youth are happy to let their DCS allowance grow and only request various amounts as they need something like a bicycle repair while others choose to request their money as soon as it is available every month. Consider withdrawing your DCS allowance and moving it into your own bank account. Why should the placement make the interest on that money instead of you? You've possibly looked forward to allowance because there are entertainment purchases you have wanted to make as soon as possible. When your own income becomes a part of your transition from semi to full independence you will have to think about delaying some entertainment purchases in favor of more practical purchases. Do you really need a version eight phone when your version seven still works? Moving out on your own means rent, bills, food, clothes, transportation and, yes, entertainment. Who is to say you don't deserve the latest phone? Maybe you can skip a couple restaurant meals and eat at home to save money this month in preparation for buying the phone and your budget will endure without skipping a beat. You've approached goals many times over in semi-independent living and you will continue to set goals and strive to meet them, making adjustments as you go, just like you did when assessing your goals required a full meeting with all your supports sitting around the table. Being responsible doesn't mean being boring, definitely plan ahead and work on a budget that covers things you need and things you want. A good rule of thumb about savings is that you should strive to have enough money saved so you could get by for two months without your current income. Sit down and sketch out a scenario where you lose your job and have to find work while paying bills. Ask your team who could help you respond to this hypothetical situation. Plan for the worst but hope for the best. You're going to be OK.

Feed the Pig
American Institute of Certified Public Accountants
http://www.feedthepig.org

Paying Taxes

Every youth gets paid for the first time and takes a minute to mentally digest their paystub. What are all these deductions? If you've kept your AHCCCS going then you don't have to worry about healthcare deductions yet but you are paying income taxes. You choose a withholding when you are hired and depending on how much you paid the state and federal governments by the end of the year, you may get some money back when you pay your taxes. This is called a tax refund. If you did not pay enough then you may owe taxes. With your first few jobs you will probably not make enough money to owe additional taxes at the end of the year. Don't worry, your income will grow as you do, and you will make more money if that is your goal. But for now get used to the idea of paying taxes on income, assets, and purchases and understand why you do. As a community of citizens, we have decided that there are common goods and services we all need, share and fund. For example, law enforcement is maintained by taxes. You're going to pay property taxes that fund public education whether you have school aged children or not. Collectively, this is beneficial to society. Crime remains lower when everybody is provided for and neighborhoods become safer as a result. If you do not agree with how your taxes are being spent then your best bet is to get involved with the political process. You can determine a new direction for public funding by voting for candidates whose values align with your own or by yourself running for elected office. In your lifetime, you will probably get the chance to vote on whether the government should provide healthcare for every citizen or not (currently does not). Maybe you have strong opinions on foreign aid and defense spending. You live here and you get a say.

InCharge
Debt Solutions
https://www.incharge.org/

IRS
Filing Your Taxes
https://www.irs.gov/filing

VOTE.org
Register to Vote
https://www.vote.org

Money Strategies

Depending on what you're trying to accomplish financially, you may find yourself one day seeking a loan in addition to your income, your tax refund, and your earned rewards. Somebody may have once told you to read the fine print. To take that very literally means to look at the tiny words at the bottom of the offer you are reading. Maybe you bought something and only when you tried to return it learned you couldn't because of a contract you agreed to but did not read. Did you ever read the contract that came on the screen when your video game console needed a firmware and software update or did you just press OK to keep going? Definitely understand everything you are agreeing to when dealing with money. Some loans may use your vehicle as collateral. That means if you don't pay back the lender they can take away your car and keep it! The lender may have enticed you into that deal by saying, "You paid for your car now shouldn't your car work for you?" Try to avoid payday loans at all costs or at least seek more education about them elsewhere. See if whatever you're trying to buy has a layaway plan. Try to pay cash before using credit but know credit has its place. For example, maybe you want braces or sometime in your life your child needs braces. Braces are a cosmetic dental procedure which means your insurance probably won't help with the cost. Often times purchasing braces requires a payment plan where the overall cost is much lower if you agree to fewer but larger payments. You may choose to put this purchase on a credit card to get the full payment to the orthodontist out of the way and then make the credit card payments on time. You will become more experienced with money through trial and error. Stay in a safe place of trial and error by always relying on your discipline, planning ahead, saving, and independent living skills. You may arrive at a place where you want to learn about investing. Investing may mean purchasing stocks. Youth who have become young adults may choose to buy common stock because of capital appreciation. That means they purchased a small piece of a company when the price is low in hopes of selling it to somebody else when the price is high. If this interests you then you should start learning money terms associated with what will become your financial portfolio. You may be in your first job but you are already working toward big goals. Do something every day that will serve and enrich your future.

DailyWorth
Top 8 Free Savings Apps
https://www.dailyworth.com/posts/3745-top-8-free-savings-apps

The Motley Fool
Investing
https://www.fool.com

SOCIAL LIFE

Meaningful Relationships

Family

Your family is an important part of your life. Hopefully you moved into semi-independent living knowing what the court imposed boundaries are around spending time with your family. If not make sure to ask your team. Many youth have some degree of unsupervised visitation rights with family, and use the opportunity of living in a semi-independent placement to rebuild relationships with loved ones. Youth with the ability to spend overnights with their family usually take care of their responsibilities during the week and head home to family on the weekend. At this point, individual and family therapy, if involved, could be working on what your important relationships will look like post-discharge. This could be a good time to locate resources that might help you if you have relationship conflict while living on your own. If you're returning to a home environment with young family members or are even a parent yourself then it might be helpful to be aware of the related community supports. Think about your emotional wellbeing while planning your discharge and raise every concern, not just where to live, work and go to school, with your team.

Kaity's Way
PEACE   Patience   Empathy   Acceptance   Caring   Equality
http://www.kaitysway.org/

Emerge! Center Against Domestic Abuse
http://www.emergecenter.org/

Strong Families AZ
Free Birth to 5 Support
http://strongfamiliesaz.com/

Diaper Bank of Southern Arizona
http://www.diaperbank.org/

Friends

Friendships no doubt make up a significant portion of your natural supports. While living in a more structured environment, you grew accustomed to weaving your time with friends into your allotment of time off-site. When suddenly living on your own, your time for friends is only limited by work, school and sleep. Conversely, monitor that you actually are spending time with friends as you adapt to your fully independent schedule. You may find that it was easier to spend time with friends while living in placement and going to high school versus living on your own and working and possibly going to college, too. Most adults don't keep friends effortlessly, and you may have to work to maintain rewarding friendships. By now, you're hopefully associating with good friends that don't try to steer you toward trouble. However, even if your friends aren't as mature as you are, you can still hang out with people who are still figuring out life skills you already mastered. Just think about consequences and protect your ability to pursue your goals. If you try dating, especially online dating, make safe choices and don't invite a new person into your home without thoroughly vetting them. A good first date is an outing that doesn't demand more than a 30 minute investment of time. You can leave a coffee shop or park faster than a restaurant or movie, and get out of both having spent less money. If you want to see the person again you can always plan a longer, more exciting second date.

OkCupid
Free Dating
http://okcupid.com

A message about pornography:

Decide for yourself if widely available Internet porn is moral or not but know that access to Internet porn has been around long enough for studies on it to emerge. Some research says consuming pornography may condition you to prefer it over pursuing real relationships. As with any addiction, your brain may become dependent on the rush associated with seeking and finding new stimulating pornography. You may someday find yourself having to break an Internet porn habit to improve the personal relationships that are important to you. Again, decide for yourself but get educated on the risks.

Your Brain on Porn
https://yourbrainonporn.com/

The Great Porn Experiment
TEDx Talks
https://youtu.be/wSF82AwSDiU

Community

While you inevitably had to come up with ways to pass time some days in placement, you should continue pursuing your hobbies and interests after semi-independent living. There are many ways young people in the community pursue leisure, including parks, zoos, museums, sports, art, music, coffee shops, restaurants, and day trips. Exploring the community is a great way to make new friends or spend time with existing friends. Find social calendars online or at the library. You could walk up and down University Boulevard and Fourth Avenue and find trivia, music, billiards and sports to enjoy watching or participating in with others. Volunteering may no longer be your go-to resume building activity but you may still find it valuable and rewarding. Playing video games doesn't have to be an isolating hobby if you involve yourself in tournaments around town. You don't have to go out and stay active in the community but if you start living on your own and feel like more of a shut in than you anticipated or just get occasionally lonely then know you can open your door and connect with friendly and safe events all over town. Living in the desert also means you are surrounded by beautiful and available scenery. Pack plenty of water and take on a trail. Where would you go to learn how to camp and fish? Staff at Summit Hut or the Sportsman Warehouse would love to answer your questions. If you have an idea percolating, put a day on your calendar to actually sit, research, call your friends and plan something. Adventure doesn't always fall on your lap but it's out there. The community offers an unlimited opportunity for fun.

Meet Up
https://www.meetup.com/

Bookmans Entertainment Exchange
Events
http://bookmans.com/events/

Reddit
The Front Page of the Internet
http://www.reddit.com

Social Media

Internet Safety

Facebook drama is ubiquitous in teen social circles. You may have participated in some online drama from time to time. Be aware that each computer has its own permanent address on the world wide web and you are never anonymous when posting online, sending email, or browsing a web page. Jokes about bombs and death threats may result in a visit from law enforcement. Aside from being mean, cyberbullying is traceable and laws are adapting to bring more severe punishments to those who engage in it. Good for you for never having been a youth who uses their online presence to harass others or for being a youth who learned from past experiences on the Internet and made a choice to act more maturely in the future. If you were the victim of cyberbullying you may have opted to delete the associated social media accounts and start new ones. Ways to protect yourself include familiarizing yourself with privacy settings, using throwaway accounts when appropriate, keeping separate email addresses for one-time registrations or junk mail, not publishing your full name and home address, finalizing Craigslist transactions in public places, using PayPal instead of your credit card as much as possible, and clearing your computer and devices of malware and spyware. Be aware that normal web browsing can pull malicious software into your system that runs in the background and compromises your private data. If your desktop computer performance seems clunky then some of this unwanted bloat may be running without you ever having installed it. You can breathe new life into an old computer and make it safe again by reformatting its hard drive and installing a free open source operating system. All you need to get started is an Internet connection, a piece of rewritable media (like a blank CD/DVD or USB memory stick), and a backup location for important files you intend to save.

Ninite
Open Source Software Installer
https://ninite.com/

LinuxMint
Open Source Operating System
https://www.linuxmint.com/

Ubuntu
The Leading Open Source Operating System
https://www.ubuntu.com/

Considerations while Posting Online

While we touched on the harmful risk of cyberbullying, there are also social risks involved in everyday non-lawbreaking posting. Consider the consequence of posting your strong political opinions on the same Facebook page where you have listed which company employs you. Or whether you remembered to change out of your work uniform before attending a party where other people posted photos. Many employers want to protect their brand by not associating with anything controversial. Having a marijuana leaf banner on your social media may catch the attention of your human resource department the next time you post to your friends that you're working until 5 o'clock and name the business. Logging into social media means algorithms are combing through your every move and indexing your likes, dislikes, and comments to grow the network and sell advertising. You don't even have to do anything intentionally bad to cast yourself in a negative light. A proactive approach is best so use social media with a heightened sense of awareness. Come up with a mental filter such as whether or not you'd feel comfortable reading that post to your boss or closest family member before you send it. Once you put something on the Internet it is there forever. Deleted web pages are viewable right now in Google's cache files. If you think you've witnessed something illegal on the Internet or something happened online that makes you feel unsafe, know that you can take your concerns directly to law enforcement. If law enforcement investigates your complaint it will follow many electronic trails. Having clicked "like" on a photo that includes a crime may put you in a compromising position. Keep using your best judgment as you enjoy social media for all of its positive convenience and fun.

Federal Bureau of Investigation
Internet Crime Complaint Center
https://www.ic3.gov/complaint/default.aspx

A message about sex trafficking:

Red Flags of a Pimp: Easily jealous, controlling/violent, promises are "too good to be true," always knows ways to make lots of money, flashes money, vague about job, encourages sexual photos and dancing for money, projects financial responsibility, demanding about sex.

Red Flags of a Victim: Older boyfriend/"Daddy" figure, new expensive items, sudden change in behavior, separation from friends and family, acting out, multiple cell phones, running away, signs of abuse, tattoos/brands, not free to come and go, fear/anxiety/depression, changing in vocabulary (Ex. The Game/Life, wifey, sister in law, tricks, or track).

Recruitment Methods: Posing as a professional, posing as a boyfriend, posing as a friend, online/social media. Facebook and Instragram, dating sites and on the back pages still - they advertise in "personal massages" since most of the others have been censored.

Quick Trip (QT) is a "safe place" for any victim seeking help. They can go to a worker and say "safe place" and the police will immediately be called to help them.

National Human Trafficking Resource Center
https://humantraffickinghotline.org/
1 (888) 373-7888
233733 (Text "HELP" or "INFO")

Offline Reputation

To leave your semi-independent placement successfully means you put a lot of effort into your goals and building your personal brand. Near the end of your stay, you probably enjoyed a lot of trust with your staff and felt many of the interactions were more social than professional. You most likely gained that trust by always being where you said you would be, cleaning up after yourself, helping out when available, and showing respect to your peers even when they were testing boundaries with you, each other, and staff. Trust takes time to build and can take even more time to rebuild. Maybe you lost trust once by bringing contraband into the house and getting caught. Your staff most likely didn't change into thinking you are a bad person but you probably had to work harder to get back to them not suspecting you during one of those often comical witch hunts that occasionally erupt whenever more than a few people live together. Trust is like a piece of paper. A piece of paper, once folded and wrinkled, can be smoothed out but never completely new again. Somebody could be cursing loudly in a store and walk around an aisle and bump into their teacher who is shopping on a weekend. All of us act differently when with friends, family, coworkers, bosses, children and other audiences but we hope our behaviors always reflect our core values. Your reputation is an important resource as you try to make it in this world.

Coaching Positive Performance
13 Simple strategies for building trust
http://www.coachingpositiveperformance.com/13-simple-strategies-building-trust/

Growth and Change

Travel and Passport

Maybe you have outgrown your community and want to do some traveling. First of all, regarding moving, be aware that leaving the state that reviews your dependency case may change your benefits and entitlements. If you're just going on vacation then make sure you've done your research. How are you getting there? What do you need to bring? Do you have time off from work? What is the weather? Who are you going with? Where will you stay? Who needs to know you are going? If you're going for an extended number of days does a neighbor need to look over any of your responsibilities? Do you have pets, plants, mail, or any chore requiring daily attention? Visiting Mexican border towns doesn't always require a passport but the laws there are different than they are in the United States. The police treat you differently. Sanborn's is a company operating in Arizona that sells vehicle insurance for traveling through Mexico. Don't count on the people you meet South of the border to speak English. You are a guest in their country. Wherever you go, the US State Department website can advise you of conditions facing tourists. Sometimes travel warnings are issued. The US has many embassies, or permanent diplomatic missions, all over the world and while visiting other countries you can find the embassy building and register your visit. Traveling is fun and exciting, and can add fulfillment to your life. Your country is a diverse landscape with many rich historical sites to visit. Perhaps pick some close landmarks to gain experience traveling. When you're ready for a passport you can submit an application to the Consolidated Justice Court downtown between 8 a.m. and 3 p.m. Just like your driver's license, you'll have to follow the steps given in the application and acquire all the associated documentation before finally having a photo taken and your passport issued.

Pima County Clerk of the Court
Passport Applications (side bar)
http://www.cosc.pima.gov/

United States Department of State
International Travel
https://travel.state.gov/content/travel/en.html

The Next Five Years

You may have noticed that when you're small, the time between Christmas and birthdays can feel like an eternity. As you age (and you probably aren't there yet), the holidays and milestones fly by in a blink. That is because at five years old, a year is a whopping one fifth of your life. At 25 years old, a single year is a much smaller sliver of your total years lived. You probably have more in common with your parents when you are 30 and they are 60, than you did when you were ten and they were 40. Or ten and 25. High school may have felt like forever while there but then you turn around and get invited to your five year high school reunion. So what are you doing with all this life and untapped potential? That is for you to decide. If you have only recently left semi-independent living and are feeling stagnant, maybe you should take a personality test to help uncover your passions. You may not hear your calling until you try more things and get more life experience. Sometimes frustrated youth in placement need to be reassured that the reality they are experiencing, with its up and downs, is not permanent. Your life is your own. Hopefully, with acknowledgement that living in a placement was never your first choice, your experience in semi-independent living was pleasant. Either way, this is the truth: Life gets better. Your life won't always be easy, and you will have to overcome challenges, but as long as you focus on little goals that build toward bigger goals you will feel a sense of power and control over your situation.

The Meyers and Briggs Foundation
Take the MBTI Instrument
http://www.myersbriggs.org/my-mbti-personality-type/take-the-mbti-instrument/

CNN Heroes
http://edition.cnn.com/specials/cnn-heroes

Glassdoor
Job Search and Company Reviews
https://www.glassdoor.com/index.htm

Life Goals

This guidebook is not a roadmap to success but hopefully you learned or can reference something useful from it when needing to work on your health and wellness, education, housing and transportation, employment, banking and saving, and social life. Whereas youth services wind down and close, a relationship with a mentor can endure past turning 18. Sometimes discharging down from a more intensive program to a mentor is a good way to maintain success without all the paperwork and monitoring that goes with a clinically observed program. You may benefit from entering a mentor program between the ages of 12 and 17 so you have somebody who has been there before when you need advice as a young adult. A mentor is just a responsible adult who is determined to provide casual guidance and support to a young person seeking it, usually having overcome similar challenges in their own life. Maybe you won't be needing full on adult services in the years to come but the difference between stumbling through your goals or reaching them more smoothly could be a trusted voice on the other end of the phone or somebody you can meet with intermittently. As you work toward, revise, and complete your goals, utilize all your independent living skills and continue reaching out to trusted sources for feedback, ideas and praise. Thanks for working so hard, you deserve all the success in the world.

Star 200 Trend Tracker
Best Industry Companies
http://dynamic.azstarnet.com/star200/

Goodwill Southern Arizona
Good Guides Youth Mentoring
http://www.goodwillsouthernaz.org/programs-and-services/goodguides-youth-mentoring/

James Potter House
http://vqarizona.com/james-potter-house

www.ingramcontent.com/pod-product-compliance
Lightning Source LLC
Chambersburg PA
CBHW072140280526
45788CB00002B/718